Falling Leaves Lap Quilt

By Pam Lindquist

Capture falling leaves in a cozy quilt to cuddle under on crisp autumn days. Quilting the panels before joining them with binding strips on the side is an easier way to manage the weight of the quilt at the machine.

FINISHED SIZE
63 x 76 inches

MATERIALS
Yardages are for 44/45-inch-wide fabrics.

- 3 yards medium brown print for strip panels
- 1¾ yards green stripe for strip panel borders, block borders and quilt binding
- 1½ yards total assorted autumn-colored prints for leaves
- 1½ yards total assorted off-white prints for leaf block backgrounds
- 5⅛ yards green or brown print for quilt backing
- 21 (3½-inch) squares tissue paper for paper-piecing the stems
- 80 x 84-inch piece batting or 16½ yards of 20-inch-wide batting
- All-purpose thread to match fabrics
- Walking foot (optional)
- Basic sewing tools and equipment

***Notes:** Preshrink and press all fabrics before cutting. Use ¼-inch-wide seams to piece the leaf blocks and panels. All other seams are ½ inch wide unless otherwise noted.*

CUTTING

- From the medium brown print, cut four 10 x 76-inch strips. From the remaining fabric, cut two 10 x 42-inch strips. From these, cut a total of six 9½ x 10-inch rectangles.
- From the green stripe, cut the following strips across the fabric width: 12 strips each 2 x 42 inches for the vertical strip-panel binding and eight strips each 3 x 42 inches for the quilt binding. Cut six strips each 1 x 42 inches. From these strips, cut (24) 1 x 9½-inch strips for the sashing strips between the leaf blocks.
- From the backing fabric, cut seven 10 x 84-inch strips.
- From the assorted autumn-colored prints, cut (21) ¾ x 4¼-inch rectangles for leaf stems, (42) 4-inch squares for half-square-triangle units and (63) 3½-inch squares for the leaf blocks.
- From the assorted off-white prints, cut (42) 4-inch squares for half-square-triangle units, (21) 3½-inch squares for the block corners, (42) 2¼ x 4¼-inch rectangles for leaf stem squares and (21) 2 x 9-inch rectangles for the leaf-block side strips.
- From the batting, cut seven strips each 10 x 84 inches.

Falling Leaves Lap Quilt

ASSEMBLY

1. Draw a ¼-inch-wide stem diagonally on each tissue-paper square. Center a ¾ x 4¼-inch stem strip right side up over the drawn line on the tissue-paper pattern (Figure 1).

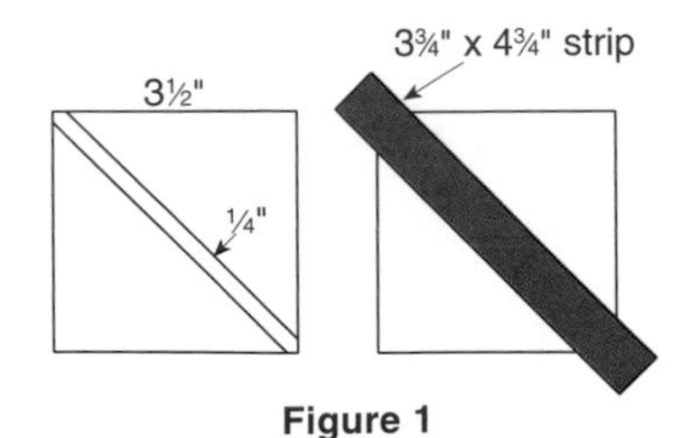

Figure 1
Draw stem on tissue; center strip over lines.

2. Align a 2¼ x 4¼-inch off-white fabric rectangle with raw edges even and right sides together along an edge of the leaf stem. Pin in place. Stitch ¼ inch from the raw edges through the fabrics and the tissue paper. Flip the fabric onto the tissue paper and press (Figure 2).

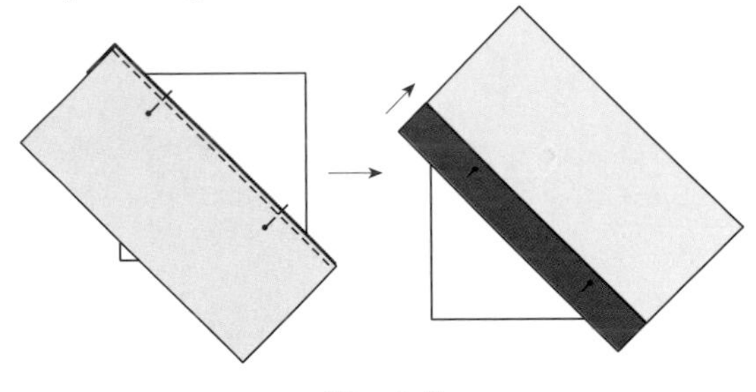

Figure 2
Add background rectangle.

3. Align a second 2¼ x 4¼-inch off-white fabric rectangle, right sides together, along the remaining raw edge of the stem. Sew in place, flip and press (Figure 3). Make a total of 21 stem squares in this manner.

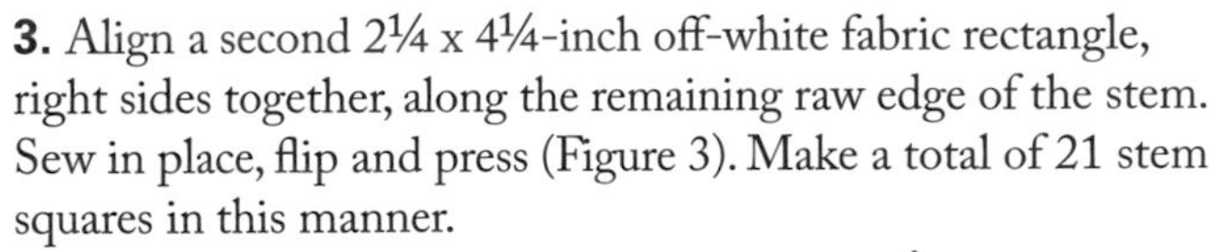

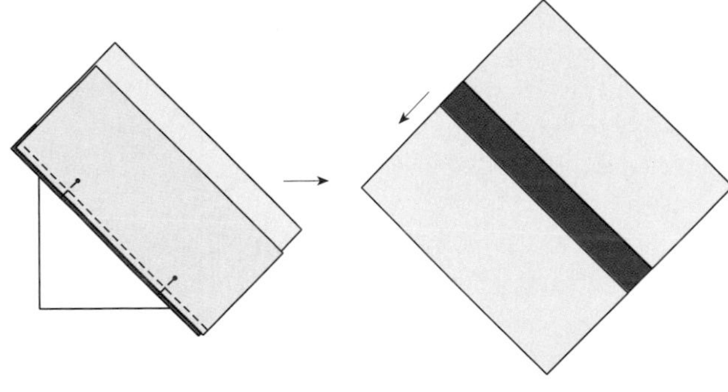

Figure 3
Make 21 stem squares.

4. Flip the piece over and use the tissue-paper edges as a guide to trim the block to 3½ inches square (Figure 4). Carefully tear away the tissue paper.

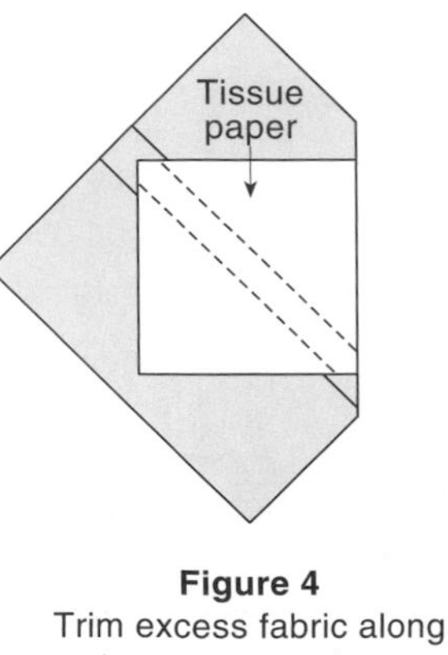

Figure 4
Trim excess fabric along tissue-paper edges.

5. Pair a 4-inch autumn print square with an off-white 4-inch square and place right sides together. Use a pencil and ruler to draw a diagonal line from corner to corner on the wrong side of the lighter square. Stitch ¼ inch from the drawn line on each side and cut apart on the line to yield two units. Flip the darker triangle toward the seam allowance and press. Trim each unit to 3½ inches square (Figure 5).

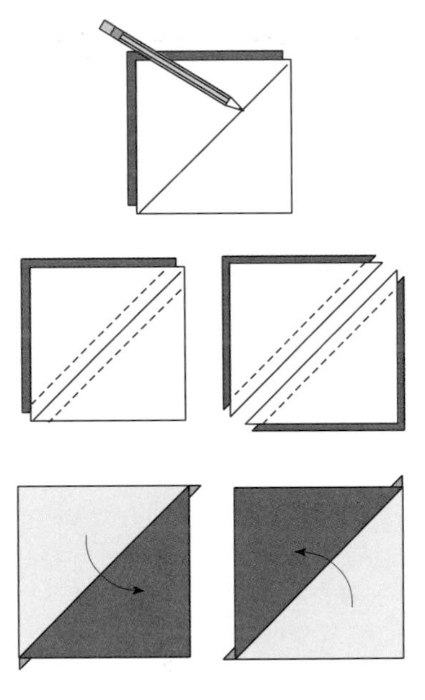

Figure 5
Make half-square triangles.

6. Arrange four 3½-inch half-square-triangle units with three autumn print 3½-inch squares, one 3½-inch off-white square and one 3½-inch leaf-stem square as shown in Figure 6 on page 4. Sew together in horizontal rows and press as directed by the arrows. Sew the rows together to complete the block. Repeat steps 5 and 6 to make a total of 21 Autumn Leaf blocks.

Falling Leaves Lap Quilt

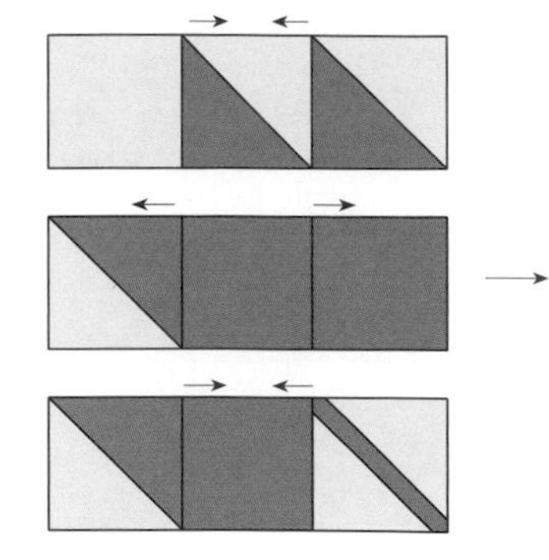

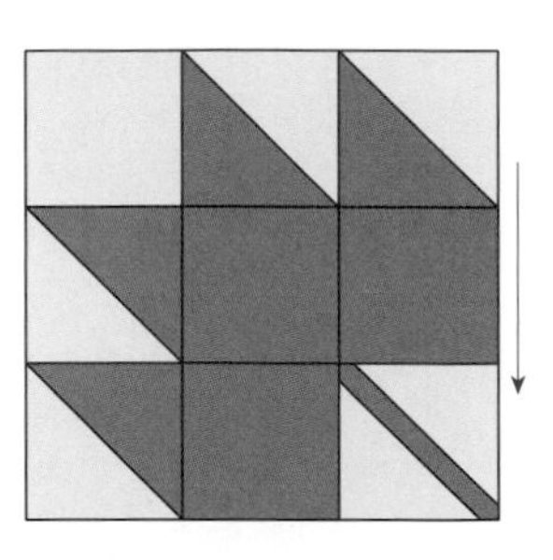

Figure 6
Make 21 Autumn Leaf blocks.
Press seams in direction of arrows.

7. Sew a 2 x 9-inch off-white rectangle to the right edge of nine Autumn Leaf blocks and to the left edge of the remaining 12 leaf blocks. Press as directed (Figure 7).

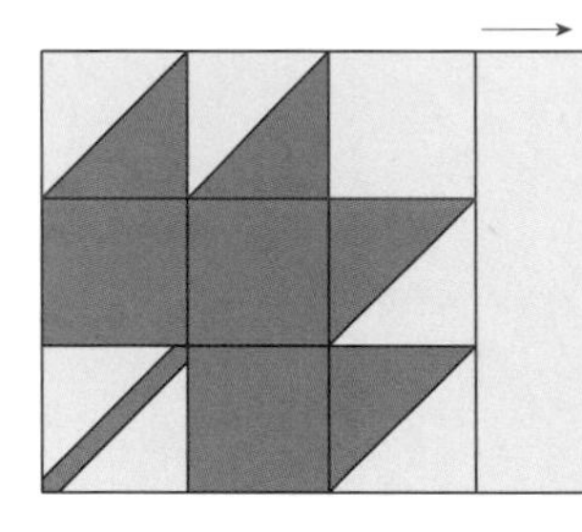

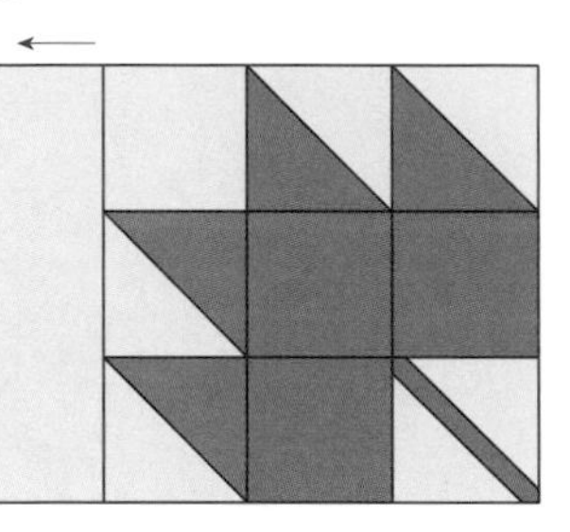

Figure 7
Add strips and press.

8. Arrange the leaf blocks in three rows with stem positions alternating as shown and 1 x 9½-inch striped sashing strips positioned between the blocks and at the top and bottom of each row. Add a 9½ x 10½-inch brown rectangle to the top and bottom of each row (Figure 8). Sew the pieces together in rows, using ¼-inch-wide seams. Press the seams toward the sashing strips.

Figure 8
Make 3 strips.

9. To prepare each panel for quilting, place a backing panel face down and add a batting strip. Smooth the leaf panel in place on top and pin or hand-baste the layers together. Quilt as desired. Trim the quilt batting and backing even with the edges of the pieced panel.
10. Layer and quilt the brown print panels in the same manner. Trim the quilt batting and backing even with the edges of the brown print panels. Arrange the plain and pieced panels in alternating fashion, beginning and ending with a brown panel.
11. Sew the 2-inch-wide binding strips together in pairs to make six long strips. Press the seams open and trim each strip to match the length (about 76 inches) of the quilted panels. Fold each strip in half with wrong sides together and press.
12. With backing sides together, pin a leaf panel to a brown print panel back-to-back with a brown print panel. With raw edges even, position and pin a folded strip on the right side of the autumn leaf strip panel. Stitch ½ inch from the raw edges. Trim the batting and the seam allowances to ¼ inch (Figure 9).

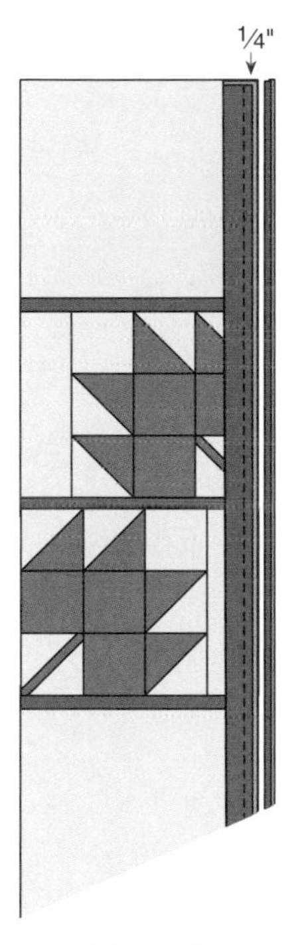

Figure 9
Stitch folded strip to layered panels. Trim to ¼".

13. Press the seam allowance and binding strip toward the brown print panel. Slipstitch the folded edge of the binding to the brown print panel (Figure 10). Repeat to join all remaining panels in the same manner.

Figure 10
Slipstitch binding to quilt.

14. Sew the 3-inch-wide binding strips together using bias seams to make one strip approximately 290 inches long. Press the seams open. Fold the strip in half lengthwise with wrong sides together and press.
15. Using a ½-inch-wide seam allowance and mitering the corners as you reach them, sew the binding to the quilt. Turn the folded edge of the binding over the raw edge of the quilt to the back and slipstitch in place, mitering the corners when you reach them. ●

Trimmed Chenille Throw

By M. J. Hoge

Soft chenille decorator fabrics have become readily available and are a wonderful choice for a cozy easy-to-sew throw. Use a decorator fabric to coordinate with your color scheme and then add beautiful trims to give this quick project design detail.

FINISHED SIZE

59 x 53 inches without fringe

MATERIALS

- 2 yards 54-inch-wide chenille decorator fabric
- 1½ yard 54-inch-wide print decorator fabric
- All-purpose sewing thread in coordinating colors
- 3 yards bullion fringe
- 3 yards flat (gimp) trim in color to coordinate with chenille (gold)
- 6 yards flat trim in color to coordinate with print fabric (green)
- Basic sewing tools and equipment

Notes: *All seams are ½ inch unless otherwise stated. Stitch with right sides together unless otherwise stated. Straighten fabric along crosswise grain before cutting. If chenille fabric frays, zigzag or serge all edges after cutting for ease of handling during construction process.*

CUTTING

- Cut two strips across width of chenille fabric each 54 x 5 inches for insets.
- Cut across width of each end of print fabric to form two pieces each 7 x 54 inches (Figure 1). ***Note:*** *The width of this strip (7-inch measurement) can be adjusted if the print design would look better with a different proportion. The 7-inch measurement worked in the photographed model because of the placement of the monkey motif. If the selected print has a one-way design, cut accordingly so that when the throw is pieced, the design will flow in the correct direction.*

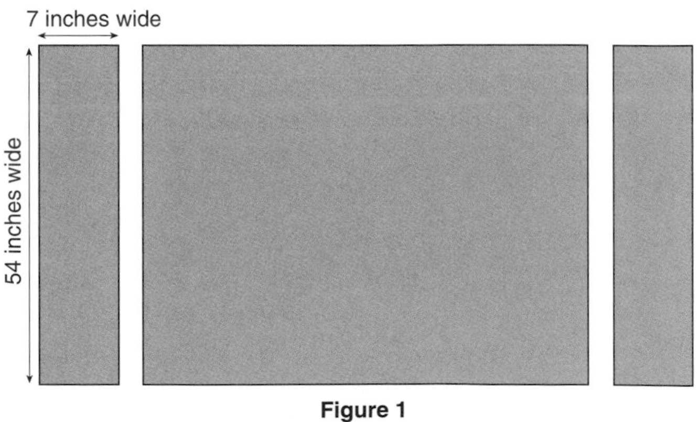

Figure 1
Cut across width of each end to form two 7 x 54" pieces.

ASSEMBLY

1. Place flat gimp trim across center of each chenille inset (Figure 2). Stitch in place with coordinating thread.

2. Place second-color trim on either side of first stitched piece, again referring to Figure 2. Stitch in place with coordinating thread color.

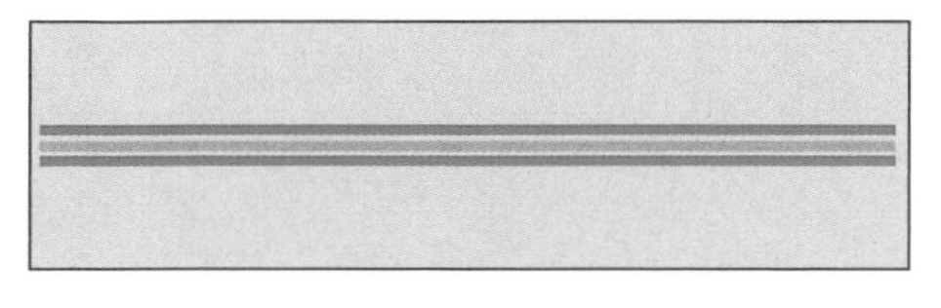

Figure 2
Stitch gimp trim in place on chenille inset.

3. Using ¼-inch seam allowance, stitch chenille insets to each end of large piece of print decorator fabric.

4. Stitch print strips to other side of chenille insets, being careful to place design in the correct direction. Press seams.

5. Place assembled print/chenille top piece and the large chenille piece together. Square the two layers to be sure they are even in size to accommodate any variation after stitching inset pieces.

6. Stitch bullion fringe to right side of each end on chenille fabric piece.

7. Stitch top piece and chenille piece together, leaving a 15-inch opening on one edge for turning.

8. Clip across corners to reduce bulk. Turn right side out and press edges.

9. Hand-stitch opening closed. ●

Cottage Flowers Lap Quilt

By Pam Lindquist

Romantic wallpaper stripes alternate with pieced squares in prints that blend together for a softly shaded quilt reminiscent of cottage-style decorating. Scalloped edges are an added delight.

FINISHED SIZE

55½ x 67½ inches

MATERIALS

Note: *Yardage is based on a fabric print that has at least three vertical floral stripes that each measure 9½ inches across. Additional yardage may be required to center the floral stripe on the quilt top in the strips. Finished size will vary based on the width of the floral stripe. Green fabric must measure at least 41 inches wide after preshrinking. If not, you will need an additional 2½ yards.*

- 44/45-inch-wide fabrics
  - 2⅞ yards wide wallpaper-stripe floral print (allows extra for print placement in the strips; also see Note)
  - ⅜ yard each 3 different light pink tone-on-tone prints for the Hourglass blocks
  - 1 yard light pink small floral print for the Hourglass blocks
  - ⅞ yard light pink medium floral print for the large squares
  - ⅞ yard light pink large floral print for the large squares
  - 5½ yards green tone-on-tone print for quilt backing and binding (see note below)
- 1 roll Airtex Roll and Quilt Batting (20 inches wide)
- 2 packages Borders Made Easy, Pattern 111 for quilting (optional)
- All-purpose thread to match fabrics
- Walking foot (optional)
- #1 safety pins for pin basting the quilt layers (optional)
- 7½-inch paper circle
- Air- or water-soluble marking pen
- Basic sewing tools and equipment

CUTTING

Notes: *Preshrink and press all fabrics before cutting. All measurements include ½-inch-wide seam allowances.*

- From the floral stripe, cut three 9½-inch wide strips along the length of the yardage. Determine the desired pattern positioning and trim the strips to 74 inches in length.
- From the light pink tone-on-tone prints for the Hourglass blocks, cut a total of eight 10¼-inch squares. Cut each square twice diagonally for a total of 32 quarter-square triangles.
- From the light pink small floral print for the Hourglass blocks, cut three strips each 10¼ x 42 inches. From the strips, cut a total of eight 10¼-inch squares. Cut each square twice diagonally for a total of 32 quarter-square triangles.
- From the light pink medium floral print, cut three strips each 8½ x 42 inches. From the strips, cut (10) 8½-inch squares.
- From the light pink large floral print, cut three strips each 8½ x 42 inches. From the strips, cut a total of (10) 8½-inch squares.
- From the green tone-on-tone print, cut a 27-inch-long piece and cut it into 3-inch-wide true-bias strips for the binding around the outer edge of the quilt. Set aside. From the remaining fabric, cut seven backing strips each 10 x 74 inches, and six vertical binding strips each 2 x 74 inches.
- From the Airtex Roll and Quilt batting, cut seven strips each 10 x 74 inches.

ASSEMBLING THE STRIP PANELS

Note: *To simplify the directions for this quilt, which includes a unique strip-quilting and assembly method, ½-inch seam allowances are used throughout. You may trim the piecing seams to ¼ inch after completing each one to eliminate the bulk and make quilting through the layers easier.*

Cottage Flowers Lap Quilt

1. Arrange two light pink tone-on-tone print quarter-square triangles with two light pink small floral print quarter-square triangles to form an Hourglass block. Using ½-inch-wide seam allowances, sew the pieces together and press as directed by the arrows (Figure 1). To eliminate bulk, trim each seam to ¼ inch before joining the units.

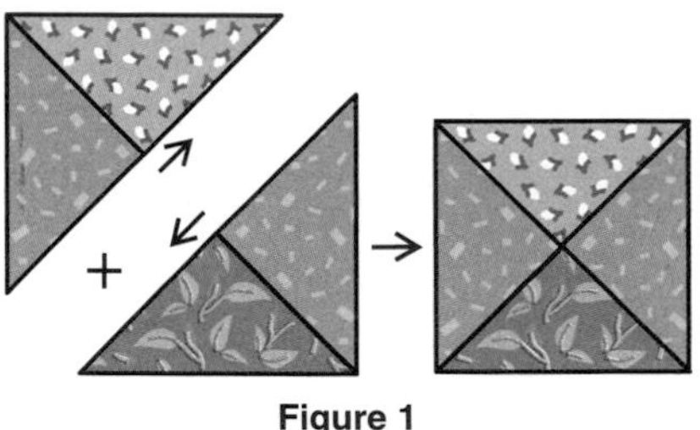

Figure 1
Make 16 Hourglass blocks.

Note: *Each Hourglass block has two matching quarter-square triangles of the light pink small floral print and two light pink tone-on-tone triangles, each one from a different print.*

2. Trim the completed blocks to measure 8½ inches square, taking care to keep the point where the seams intersect in the exact center of each block.

3. Referring to Figure 2 at right for print placement, arrange the 8½-inch medium and large floral squares with the Hourglass blocks to create four rows of nine blocks each. Sew the blocks together in each row, trim the seams to ¼ inch and press the seams in one direction.

4. To prepare each pieced strip for quilting, place a 10-inch-wide green strip face down on a large flat surface. Center a 10-inch-wide strip of batting on top. Center a pieced quilt strip face up on the batting and pin-baste the layers (or hand-baste if desired).

5. Mark the desired quilting pattern on the Hourglass strip and hand- or machine-quilt as desired. Or, follow the manufacturer's directions if you are using the Borders Made Easy quilting pattern. Trim the quilt batting and backing even with the edges of the pieced strip.

6. Layer and quilt the floral stripe panels in the same manner, using the 10-inch-wide backing and batting strips and the 9½-inch-wide floral strips.

Make 2 of each panel.

Figure 2
Pieced Strip Assembly

ASSEMBLING THE QUILT

1. Fold each 2 x 74-inch green strip in half lengthwise with wrong sides together and press.

2. Beginning and ending with a pieced strip, arrange the pieced and floral strips in alternating fashion.

3. Pin a quilted Hourglass panel back-to-back with a floral-stripe panel. With raw edges even, position and pin a folded green strip on the right side of the Hourglass strip. Stitch ½ inch from the raw edges. Trim the seam allowances, staggering the layer widths to avoid a lump under the binding.

4. Press the seam and binding strip toward the floral-stripe panel. Hand-stitch the folded edge of the binding to the floral panel.

5. Using bias seams, sew the 3-inch-wide bias binding strips together to make one strip approximately 320 inches long. Press the seams open. Fold the strip in half lengthwise with wrong sides together and press, taking care not to stretch the bias.

6. Using the 7½-inch paper circle as a pattern and an air- or water-soluble marking pen, trace a scallop at each end of each strip. Use these lines as guides for placing the raw edge of the quilt binding to create the scallops at each end of the quilt and pin in place. ***Note:*** *If you prefer, you can eliminate the scallops and finish the quilt with binding as a complete rectangle.*

7. Using a ½-inch-wide seam allowance, sew the prepared bias binding to the quilt top. Take care not to stretch the bias and ease it gently around the scallop curves. Pivot at the inner point of each scallop to miter (Figure 3).

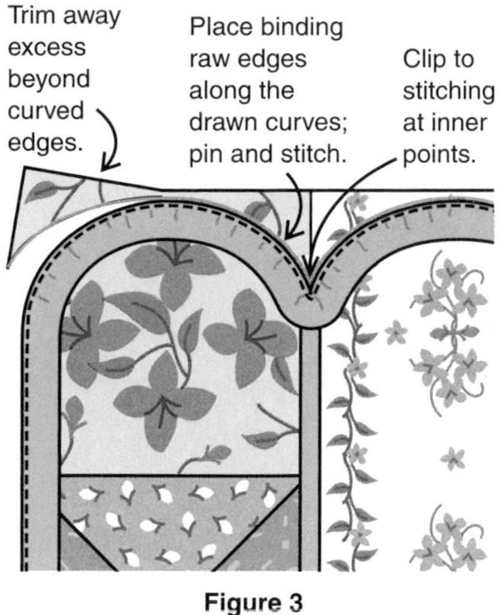

Figure 3
Sew binding to quilt.

8. Clip the inner points as needed to facilitate turning the binding over the seam edge to the underside. As you turn it, a mitered tuck will form on the front. Use a blind stitch to anchor the miter. Create a mitered fold on the back at each scallop point in the same manner. Slipstitch the folded edge of the binding to the quilt backing. ●

"Tulips All Around" Quilt

By Michele Crawford for Coats & Clark

Pretty spring tulips provided the inspiration for this lovely machine-quilted wall hanging. Use easy machine-appliqué and piecing techniques to stitch this quilt and display it just in time for warmer days.

FINISHED SIZE
38 X 38 inches

MATERIALS
- 44/45-inch-wide print fabrics
  - 1⅞ yards large white floral
  - ⅞ yard white tone-on-tone
  - ⅝ yard green scroll
  - ⅓ yard pink tone-on-tone
  - ⅓ yard yellow with pink flowers
  - ¼ yard tiny pink floral
  - ⅙ yard tiny ivory floral
  - ⅛ yard tiny green floral
  - ⅛ yard pink dot
  - ⅛ yard green dot
- 1 yard paper-backed fusible web
- 1¼ yards quilter's fleece
- Coats Dual Duty Plus All-Purpose Thread—White, Pink #31, Powder Green #58A, Primrose #72A
- Coats Rayon Thread—Pink #31, Powder Green #58A
- Coats Color Twist Thread—Buttercup #760
- Coats Dual Duty Plus Machine Quilting & Craft Thread—White, Pink #31
- Pencil
- Rotary cutter, ruler and cutting mat
- Basic sewing tools and equipment

***Notes:** Prewash the fabric before cutting. Use ¼ inch for seam allowance unless otherwise stated. Stitch pieces right sides together with all-purpose thread unless otherwise stated. Press seam allowances during construction.*

CUTTING
- From white tone-on-tone print fabric, cut four 12½-inch squares.
- From tiny pink floral print fabric, cut 12 strips each 1½ x 12½ inches.
- From tiny green floral fabric, cut nine 1½-inch squares.
- From tiny ivory floral fabric, cut 56 rectangles each 1½ x 2 inches for I rectangles in pieced border.
- From pink dot fabric, cut 28 rectangles each 1½ x 2 inches for PD rectangles in pieced border.
- From green dot fabric, cut 24 pieces each 1½ x 2 inches for GD rectangles and four 2-inch squares for corners in pieced border.
- From large white floral print, cut one 42-inch square for quilt backing.
- From the width of the yardage on the large white floral print fabric, cut two 4½ x 30½-inch strips for outside border.
- From the length of the yardage on the large white floral print fabric, cut two 4½ x 38½-inch strips for outside border and four 2¼ x 42-inch strips for binding.
- From green scroll fabric, cut one 17 x 33-inch piece.
- From pink tone-on-tone print fabric, cut one 9 x 17-inch piece.
- From yellow fabric with pink flowers, cut one 9 x 17-inch piece.

"Tulips All Around" Quilt

ASSEMBLY

1. For center section, stitch 1½-inch x 12½-inch tiny pink floral strips and 1½-inch tiny green floral squares to the white tonal squares (Figure 1).

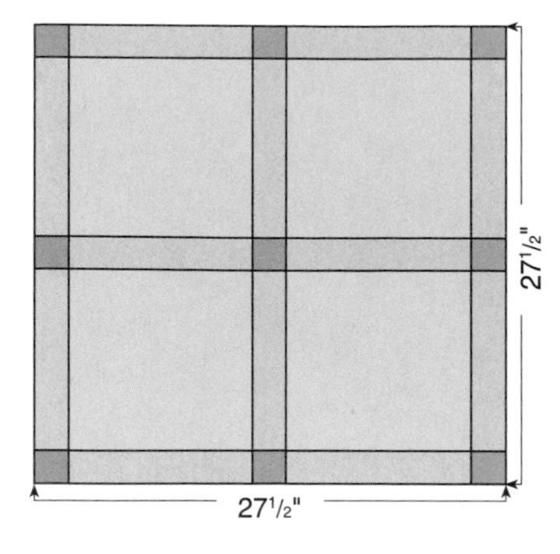

Figure 1
Stitch sashing strips to white tonal squares.

2. For pieced border, stitch I, PD and GD rectangles together (Figure 2) to make a 2 x 27½-inch strip. Repeat to make a total of four strips.

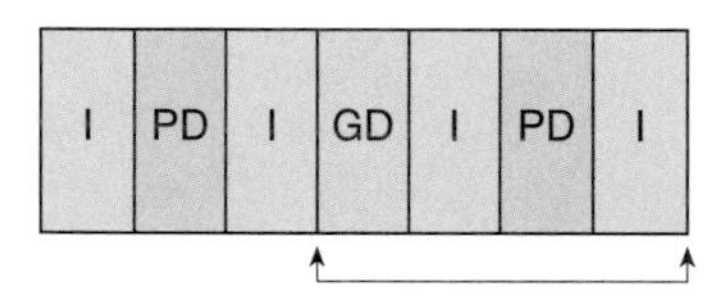

Figure 2
Repeat this section until you have a total of 27 rectangles forming a 2" x 27½" strip.

3. Stitch pieced border strips to two opposite edges of center section. Stitch a 2-inch green dot square to each end of the remaining two pieced border strips. Stitch these two strips to remaining edges of the center section and ends of first two border strips (Figure 3).

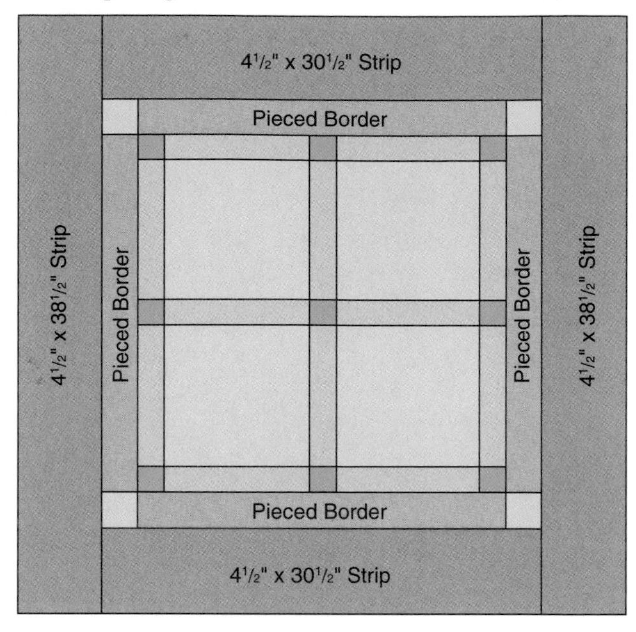

Figure 3
Add border strips.

4. Stitch a 4½ x 30½-inch large white floral strip to two opposite edges of assembled quilt center. Stitch a 4½ x 38½-inch large white floral strip to each remaining edge of the quilt center to complete quilt top, again referring to Figure 3.

5. Center a 42-inch square of fleece on wrong side of the quilt backing square. Center wrong side of the quilt top over the fleece. Pin or hand-baste layers together.

6. Use white machine-quilting thread to machine-quilt in the seam between the white tone-on-tone square and the pink print floral border strips.

7. Use pink machine-quilting thread to machine-quilt in the seams between the tiny pink floral border and the large white floral border.

8. Topstitch around outside of quilt top ⅛ inch in from the edge. Trim excess fabric and fleece.

9. For binding, stitch the four 2¼ x 42-inch large white floral strips together to make one long strip. Fold the strip in half widthwise with wrong sides together. Press.

10. Matching edges and mitering corners, stitch one long edge of the folded binding strip around front of quilt. To finish ends of binding, overlap ends and fold top end under; cut off excess ½ inch from the fold. Turn strip to back of quilt, fold edge under and hand-stitch in place.

11. Fuse web to wrong side of the green scroll 17 x 33-inch piece, the pink tonal 9 x 17-inch piece and the yellow with pink flowers 9 x 17-inch piece.

12. Trace eight each of petals appliqué and center appliqué on both the fused pink tonal fabric and the fused yellow with pink flowers fabric. Trace 16 of leaves appliqué on the fused green scroll fabric. Cut out each piece and peel off paper backing.
13. Center four of the leaves appliqués in each white tonal square as shown in photo. Fuse in place. Position two of each color of the petals appliqués and the center appliqués in each white tonal square as shown. Fuse in place.
14. With matching-color rayon threads, machine-appliqué around all appliqué pieces using a buttonhole stitch. ●

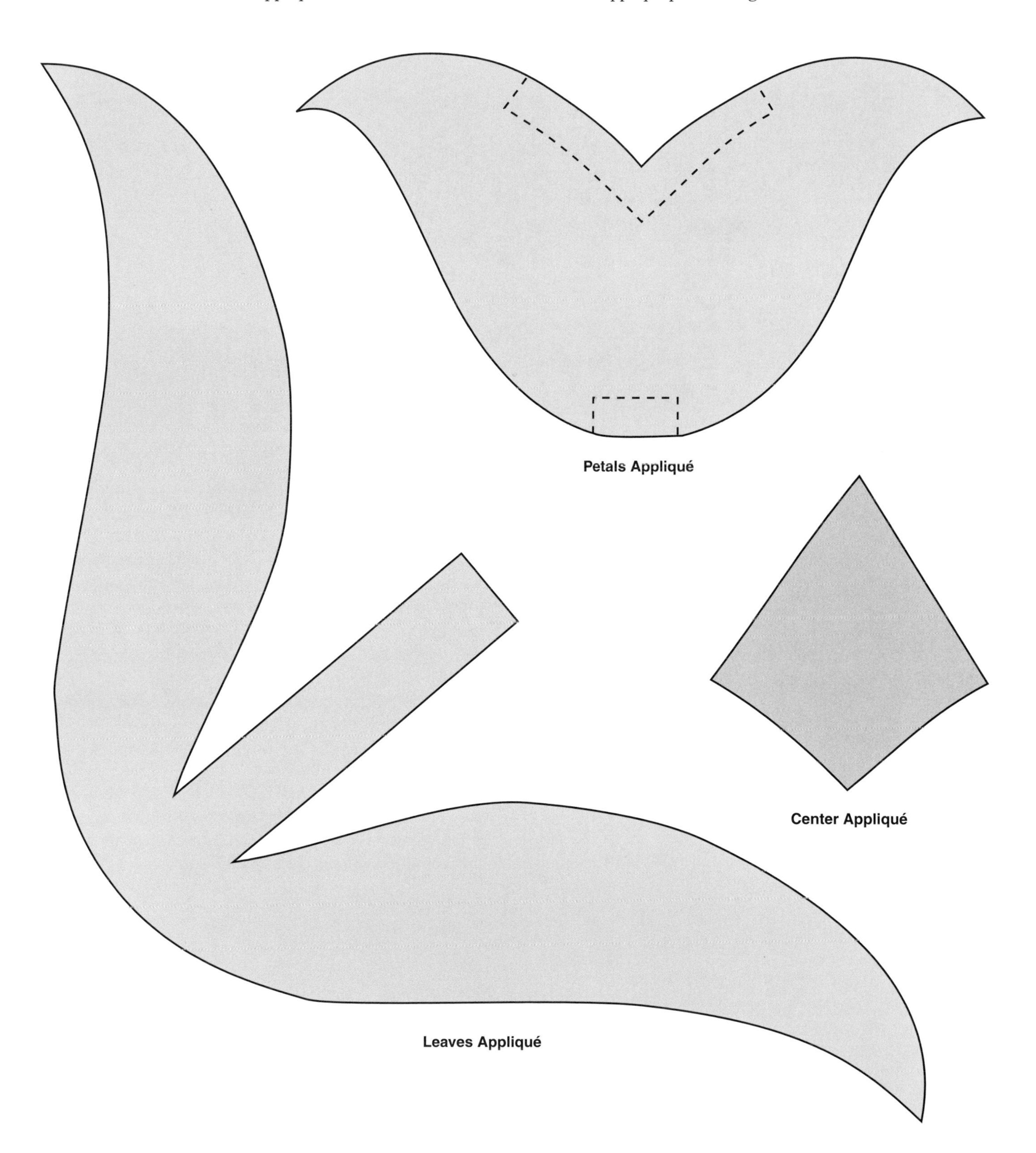

Kissy Fish Lap Quilt

By Meg Tryba

A clever twist of color placement turns the traditional Hunter's Star block into colorful tropical fish, rubbing noses in their watery background. It is a wonderful lap quilt or the perfect wall hanging for creating a focal point in a child's room.

FINISHED SIZE

54½ x 54½ inches

MATERIALS

Note: All yardages are for 44/45-inch-wide cotton.

- ¾ yard aqua tone-on-tone print for water background color
- 1 yard yellow tone-on-tone print for fish bodies and the inner and middle borders
- ⅓ yard red print for fish noses and middle border
- ⅓ yard green print for fish noses and middle border
- ¼ yard orange print for fish tails
- ¼ yard teal tone-on-tone print for fish tails
- ⅝ yard dark blue tone-on-tone print for star points
- ⅝ yard dark blue print for middle border
- 2 yards fish print for the outer border and binding
- 3¼ yards coordinating print for backing
- 60-inch square batting
- 6-inch-square rotary-cutting ruler
- Rotary cutter, mat and ruler
- All-purpose thread to match fabrics
- Basic sewing tools and equipment
- Crystals and applicator for fish eyes (optional)

CUTTING

Notes: Preshrink all fabrics and press to remove wrinkles. Strip cutting is based on a usable width of 42 inches after preshrinking. All seam allowances are ¼ inch wide unless otherwise noted.

- From the aqua tone-on-tone print, cut eight 10-inch squares. Cut the squares in half twice diagonally for 32 quarter-square triangles.
- From the yellow tone-on-tone print, cut four strips each 2 x 42 inches for inner border and eight strips each 2¼ x 42 inches wide for the fish bodies.
- From the red print, cut four strips each 1¾ x 42 inches.
- From the green print, cut four strips each 1¾ x 42 inches.
- From the orange print, cut three strips each 2 x 42 inches; crosscut a total of 16 pieces each 2 x 6 inches.
- From the teal tone-on-tone print, cut three strips each 2 x 42 inches; crosscut a total of 16 pieces each 2 x 6 inches.
- From the dark blue tone-on-tone print for the star points, cut eight strips each 2 x 42 inches wide; crosscut 64 pieces each 2 x 4½ inches.
- From the dark blue print for the pieced middle border, cut four strips each 3½ x 42 inches. From two of the strips, cut a total of eight pieces each 3½ x 10 inches.
- From the fish print, cut four border strips each 6 inches wide, cutting along the length of the yardage. For the binding, cut four lengthwise strips each 2¾ inches wide.

HOUSE OF WHITE BIRCHES, BERNE, INDIANA 46711 WWW.WHITEBIRCHES.COM

ASSEMBLY

1. Sew each of four 2¼-inch yellow tone-on-tone strips to a 1¾-inch green strip and press toward the green strip. Repeat with the remaining yellow strips and the red strips. You should have a total of eight strip units for the fish.

2. Cut triangles from the strip units, placing the point of the ruler on the red or green strip as shown (Figure 1 below). Align the edge of the body strip with the 5-inch marks on the ruler. Make the first cut to create a 45-degree angle and discard the selvage edge pieces. Cut along the adjacent edge of the ruler to create a nose-unit triangle. Carefully rotate the ruler to the other side of the strip set, and cut a second triangle. Set aside this and all other triangles cut from this edge of the strip unit for the pieced middle border. Continue rotating the ruler and cutting triangles from both sides of the strip unit. You will need 16 nose units and 12 border units from the red/yellow and the same number from the green/yellow strip sets. Mark the center of the long edge of each of the nose units (Figure 2 below).

3. Cut triangles in this same manner from the 3½ x 42-inch dark blue print strips for the pieced middle border. You will need a total of 20 dark blue print triangles. Set all triangles aside.

4. Divide the 2 x 4½-inch dark blue tone-on-tone rectangles into two stacks of 32 each. On the wrong side of a rectangle, draw a 45-degree line from one corner to the opposite long edge as shown in Figure 3. Mark 32 in this manner. On the rectangles in the second stack, draw the line from the opposite corner.

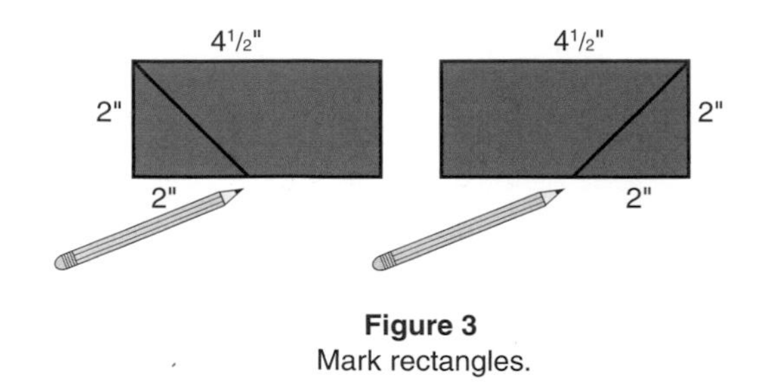

Figure 3
Mark rectangles.

5. Mark the center of one long edge on each 2 x 6-inch orange and each 2 x 6-inch teal rectangle. Place a marked blue rectangle face down at the right-hand end of each orange rectangle. Stitch on the line and trim the seam to ¼ inch. Press the seam toward the dark blue. Add a dark blue rectangle to the opposite end of the orange rectangle in the same fashion. Make 16 units. Repeat with the remaining blue rectangles and the teal rectangles for a total of 32 fish tails, 16 of each color combination (Figure 4).

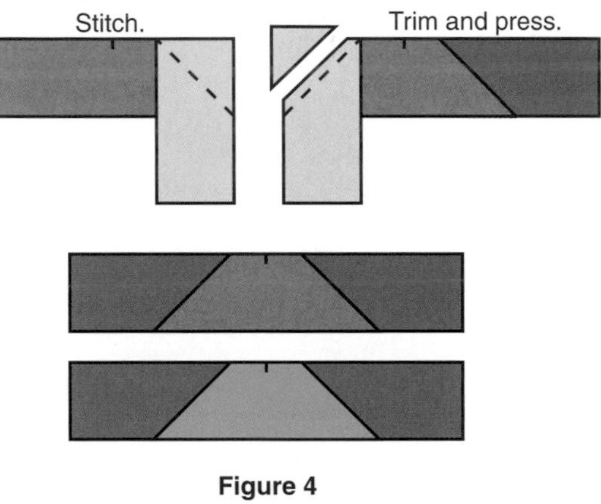

Figure 4
Make fish-tail units.

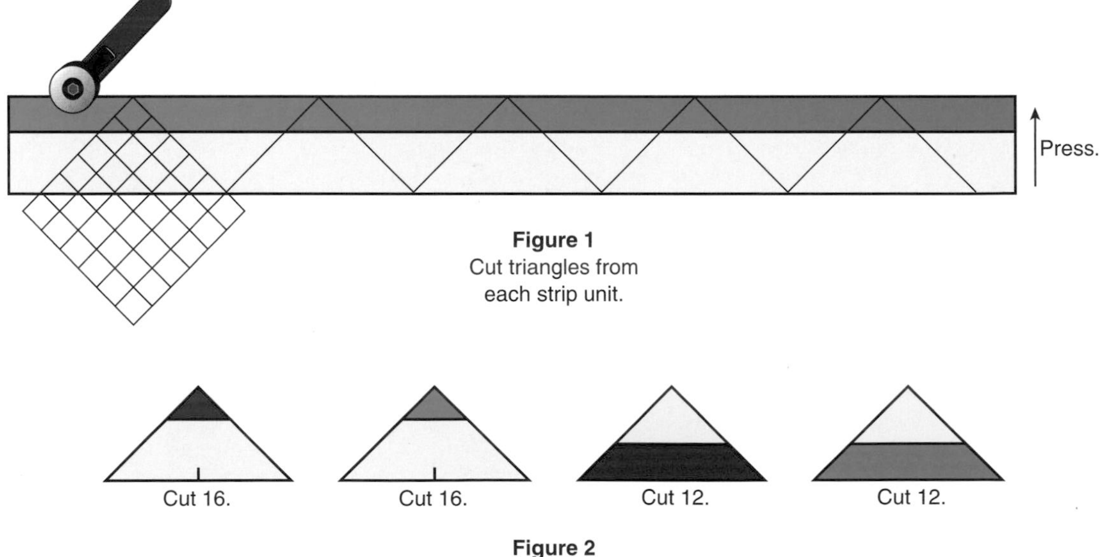

Figure 1
Cut triangles from each strip unit.

Figure 2
Mark center of each nose unit.

6. With center marks matching, sew each red nose unit to an orange tail unit. Repeat with the green nose units and the teal tail units. Press the seams toward the yellow strip in each unit (Figure 5). Trim the excess dark blue rectangle even with the triangle edges (Figure 6).

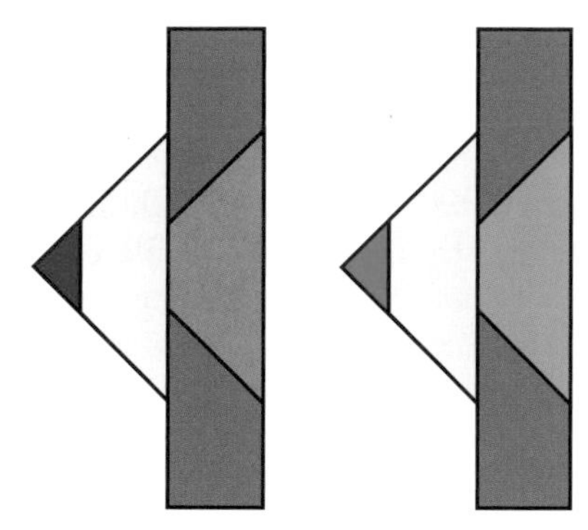

Figure 5
Sew fish tails to nose units.
Make 16 of each.

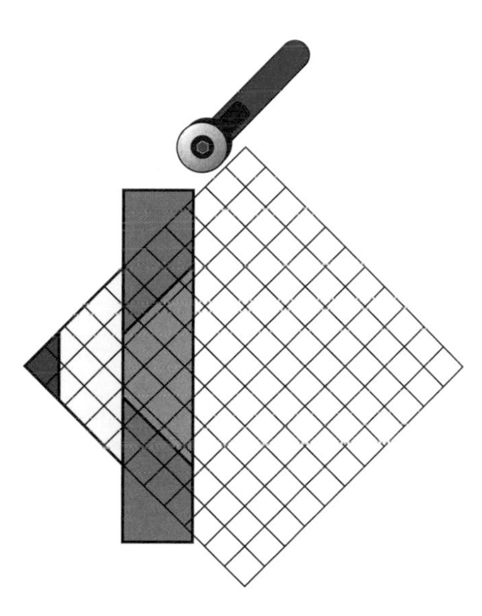

Figure 6
Trim tail units even with nose unit edges.

7. Sew an aqua background triangle to each pieced fish unit. Note that the aqua triangles are cut oversize (see Figure 7). Press the seam toward the aqua triangle. You should have a total of 32 blocks, 16 of each color combination.

8. Sew the units together in pairs to make "hourglass" blocks. Press the seams toward the aqua in each unit. To do so, carefully snip the center seam intersection so you can press the center seam in opposite directions in each block. This eliminates a bump in the center of the finished block (Figure 7).

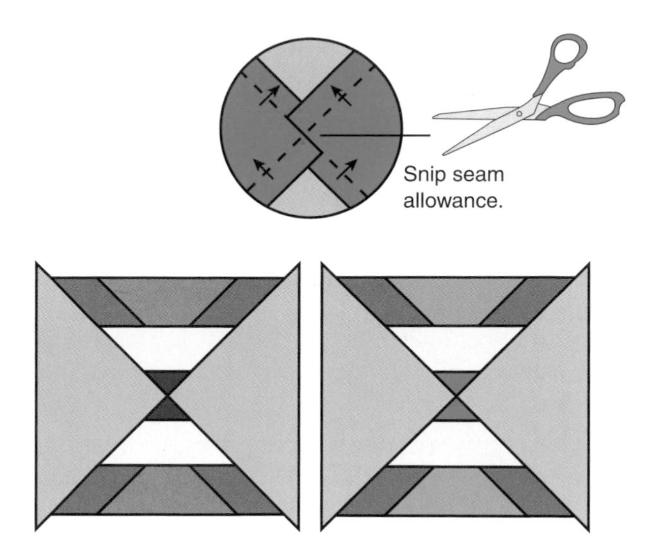

Figure 7
Complete the Kissy Fish blocks.
Make 8 of each.

9. Square blocks to 9 x 9 inches, making sure the kissing noses are centered in each one.

10. Arrange the blocks in four rows of four blocks each, rotating the position of the fish as shown in Figure 8. Sew the blocks together in rows and press the seams toward the aqua triangles in each row. Sew the rows together to create the center of the quilt top.

Figure 8
Kissy Fish Quilt Assembly

11. Make a 45-degee-angle cut at one end of each of the four 3½ x 10-inch strips of dark blue print (Figure 9).

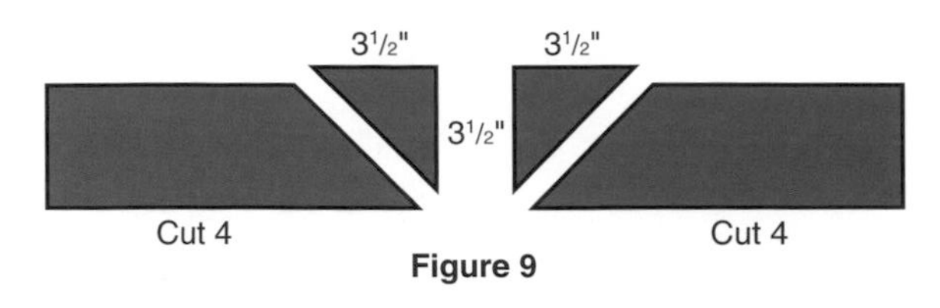

Figure 9

12. Sew triangles for the pieced middle border together as shown to make four identical strips. Add a dark blue piece from step 11 to each end (Figure 10).

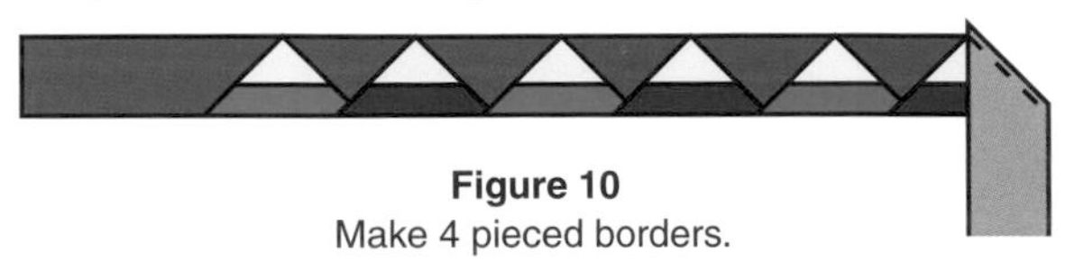

Figure 10
Make 4 pieced borders.

13. Fold each border strip (inner, middle and outer) in half and mark the centers for matching. Sew the strips together with centers matching to make four border strips. Press all seams toward the outer border in each set of borders as shown in Figure 11.

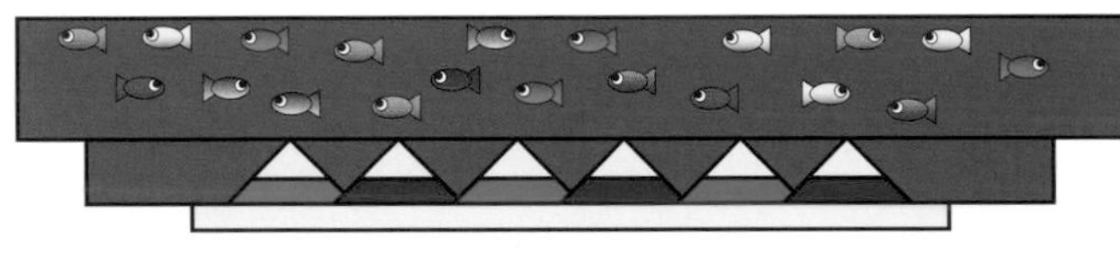

Figure 11
Sew borders together, matching centers.

14. Mark the center at each edge of the quilt top and the raw edge of the inner border on each set of borders. Measure the quilt top through the center and subtract ½ inch.
15. Mark the length determined in step 1 at the raw edge of the assembled border strip. Mark the center of the strip.

16. Carefully mark the ¼-inch seam intersection at each corner on the wrong side of the quilt top.
17. Pin a border to the quilt top with centers matching the quilt-top seam intersections. Stitch, beginning and ending the seam carefully at the seam intersections. Press the seam toward the borders. Add the remaining borders in the same manner.
18. Fold the quilt top diagonally with right sides facing and the raw edges of the adjacent border strips aligned.
19. Position a rotary ruler along the fold and across the border strips and draw the stitching line (Figure 12). Beginning at the seam intersections, stitch on the marked line. Trim the excess border ¼ inch from the stitching and press the seam open. Repeat to miter the remaining corners.

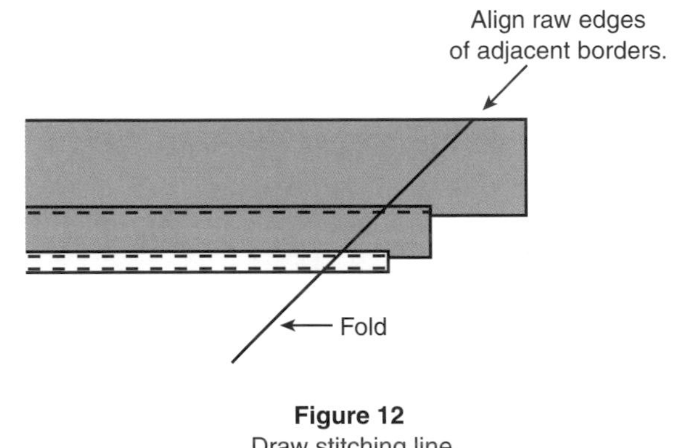

Figure 12
Draw stitching line

for mitered border.

20. Layer the quilt top with batting and backing and baste the layers together. Quilt as desired.
21. Optional: For sparkly eyes, add crystals to each fish nose with a hot-fix wand.
22. Join the binding strips with bias seams and press open. Fold the strip in half with wrong sides together and press. Bind the quilt, using a ⅜-inch-wide seam allowance. ●

Snowflake Flurries Lap Quilt

By Lucy A. Fazely and Michael Burns

Frosty silver snowflakes float against a sea of blues in this chill-chasing lap quilt. Fusible appliqué and a simple design make this an easy project to finish for gift giving or holiday decorating in your home.

FINISHED SIZE

Quilt: 52½ x 67½ inches

MATERIALS

- 44/45-inch-wide blue tone-on-tone prints
  - 1¼ yards dark blue for blocks and binding
  - ¾ yard royal blue for blocks
  - ¾ yard medium blue for blocks
  - ¾ yard light blue for blocks
  - ¾ yard pale blue for blocks
- 44/45-inch-wide prints
  - 1¼ yards silver-on-white print (snowflakes)
  - 3⅓ yards for backing
- 3¾ yards 12-inch-wide paper-backed fusible web
- Template plastic
- 4½ yards 20-inch-wide tear-away stabilizer
- 57 x 72-inch piece batting
- All-purpose sewing thread
- Clear nylon or polyester monofilament thread
- Rotary cutter, mat and ruler
- Basic sewing tools and equipment

CUTTING

Cut all strips across the fabric width.

- Cut three strips each 8 inches x fabric width from the medium, royal and dark blue prints. From these strips, cut (13) 8-inch squares of each color.
- From the remaining dark blue print, cut six strips each 2½ inches x fabric width and set aside for the binding.
- Cut three strips each 8 inches x fabric width from the pale and the light blue prints. From these strips, cut (12) 8-inch squares of each color.
- From the silver-on-white fabric, cut (40) 8-inch squares.
- From the paper-backed fusible web, cut (40) 6-inch squares.
- Trace each snowflake template on pages 24 and 25 onto template plastic. Cut out each shape.
- On the paper side of each square of fusible web, trace around a snowflake template. Trace 20 of Snowflake A and 20 of Snowflake B.
- Following manufacturer's directions, center and fuse a snowflake square to the wrong side of each silver-on-white square. Cut out each snowflake on the drawn lines. Remove the backing paper.
- From the cutaway stabilizer, cut (40) 8-inch squares.

Snowflake Flurries Lap Quilt

QUILT ASSEMBLY & FINISHING

Use ¼-inch-wide seam allowances to sew the blocks together.

1. Referring to the Quilt Diagram, arrange the blue squares in nine rows of seven squares each.

2. Center a snowflake in the square shown in the diagram. Fuse in place following the manufacturer's directions. As you complete each snowflake block, reposition it in the quilt layout.

3. Adjust the sewing machine for a short, narrow zigzag stitch and thread the needle with clear nylon or polyester monofilament thread. Use all-purpose thread in the bobbin.

4. Pin a piece of tear-away stabilizer to the wrong side of each snowflake square.

5. Zigzag around the raw edges of each snowflake. Remove the stabilizer.

6. Beginning at the top row, sew the squares together in horizontal rows. Press the seams in opposite directions from row to row (Figure 1).

Figure 1
Press seams in opposite directions from row to row.

7. Sew the rows together to complete the quilt-top assembly. Press the joining seams in one direction.

8. To make the backing, cut the backing fabric into two equal lengths. Sew the lengths together along a set of selvages to create a piece that is approximately 60 x 90 inches. Trim the piece to 60 x 75 inches. The seam in the backing will run across the narrowest dimension of the finished quilt.

9. With the backing face down, center the batting on top. Place the quilt top face up on top of the batting. Smooth out any wrinkles and pin or hand-baste the layers together.

10. Quilt as desired. Trim the batting and backing even with the quilt-top edges.

11. Using bias seams, sew the binding strips together and press the seams open. Turn under one end at a 45-degree angle and press. Trim excess, leaving a ¼-inch-wide turn-under allowance. Fold the strip in half lengthwise with wrong sides together and press (Figure 2).

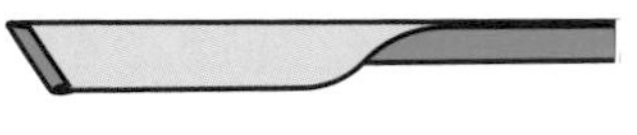

Figure 2
Prepare binding strip.

12. Beginning in the center of one long edge of the quilt and starting a few inches from the turned-under end, stitch the binding to the right side of the quilt. Use a ⅜-inch-wide seam allowance. Miter the corners as you reach them (Figure 3).

Figure 3
Stitch binding to quilt, mitering corners.

13. When you reach the beginning of the binding, trim the excess binding, allowing enough to tuck into the open end at the beginning of the binding. Complete the stitching.

14. Wrap the binding to the back of the quilt over the seam allowance and slipstitch in place, mitering the corners. The folded edge of the binding should fall along or just cover the stitching. ●

Quilt Diagram

HOUSE OF WHITE BIRCHES, BERNE, INDIANA 46711 WWW.WHITEBIRCHES.COM

Snowflake Flurries Lap Quilt

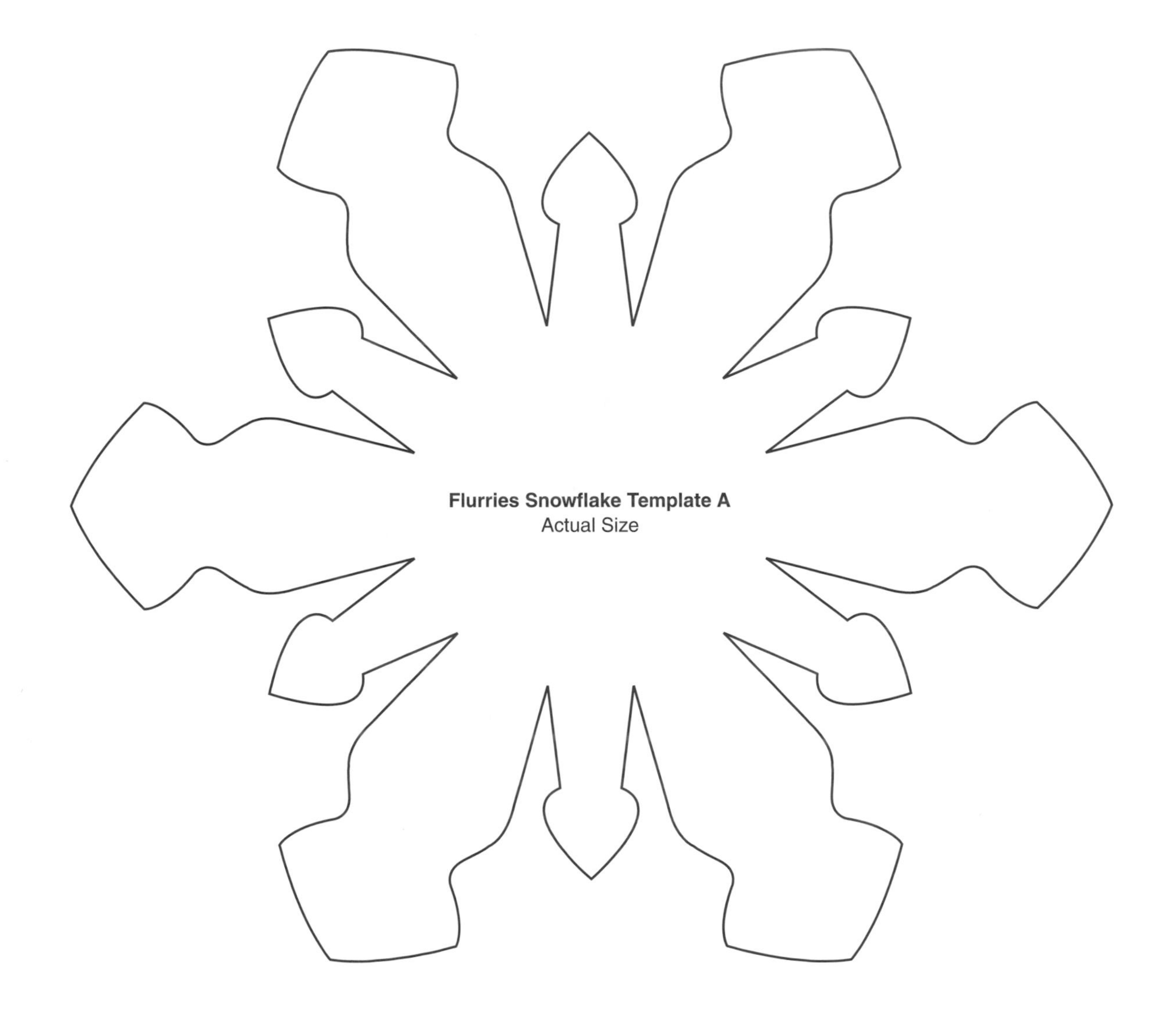

Flurries Snowflake Template B
Actual Size

Make Mine Mocha

By Pam Lindquist

Whether Dad loves mocha or not, he will appreciate his own man-size lap quilt cut from a mélange of coffee colors. The scrappy quilt features a few blocks that require easy curved piecing plus lots of big and small squares. Make a matching pillow for naptime.

FINISHED SIZES
Quilt: 63 x 81 inches
Pillow: 14 inches square

MATERIALS FOR THE QUILT
- 44/45-inch-wide fabrics
  - 8⅜ yards assorted grays and browns in light, medium and dark tones
  - 5⅜ yards brown print flannel for quilt backing
  - ⅞ yard brown print for binding
- 71 x 89-inch piece of batting

MATERIALS FOR THE PILLOW
- Assorted scraps mocha-colored fabrics (at least 7 inches square or larger)
- ⅝ yard 44/45-inch-wide brown print flannel for pillow front border and pillow back
- 16 x 16-inch piece batting
- 16 x 16-inch piece muslin
- 12-inch-long all-purpose zipper
- Freezer paper
- 14-inch square pillow form

MATERIALS FOR BOTH PROJECTS
- All-purpose thread to match fabrics
- Rotary cutter, mat and ruler
- Template plastic
- Walking foot (optional)
- Freezer paper
- Basic sewing tools and equipment

CUTTING FOR THE MAKE MINE MOCHA QUILT
Notes: *Preshrink and press fabrics before cutting. Cut all strips across the fabric width. All measurements include a ¼-inch-wide seam allowance unless otherwise stated.*

- From the assorted light, medium and dark gray and brown fabrics, cut:
  - 11 strips each 9½ x 42 inches. From the strips, cut a total of (44) 9½-inch squares.
  - 16 strips each 6½ x 42 inches. From the strips, cut a total of (96) 6½-inch squares.
  - 10 strips each 3½ x 42 inches. From the strips, cut a total of (102) 3½-inch squares.
  - Three strips each 5¼ x 42 inches. From the strips, cut a total of (19) 5¼-inch squares.
  - Four strips each 3¾ x 42 inches. From the strips, cut a total of (37) 3¾-inch squares.
- From the brown print binding fabric, cut nine strips each 3 x 42 inches.
- Trace the templates on pages 29-31 onto freezer paper. You will need 19 each of the two shapes for the 9½-inch blocks and 37 of each of the shapes for the 6½-inch squares.

HOUSE OF WHITE BIRCHES, BERNE, INDIANA 46711 WWW.WHITEBIRCHES.COM

Make Mine Mocha

QUILT ASSEMBLY

Use ¼-inch-wide seam allowances unless otherwise directed.

1. With the waxy side down, position the straight edges of 19 of Template A on the wrong side of 19 of the 9½-inch blocks. Use a dry iron to adhere the paper to the fabric. Cut along the curved edge with scissors and remove the freezer paper.

2. Press the waxy side of freezer-paper Template B onto the wrong side of the 5¼-inch fabric squares, matching the corner and straight edges. Use scissors to cut out the pieces (Figure 1). Remove the freezer-paper template.

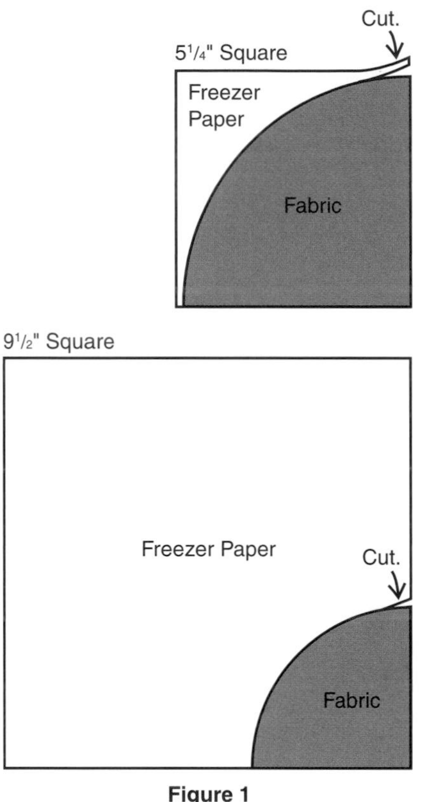

Figure 1
Apply freezer-paper templates to fabric squares.

3. Arrange pieces A and B in sets. Matching centers, pin the pieces together in each set. Work with the concave piece on top of the convex piece.

4. Stitch the pieces together and press the seams toward the quarter circle in each completed block. ***Note:*** *When you join the blocks later, you will need to press some of the seams in opposite directions to avoid bulk at the seam intersections. If you wish, you can postpone pressing until you have arranged all the pieces of the quilt (Figure 2).*

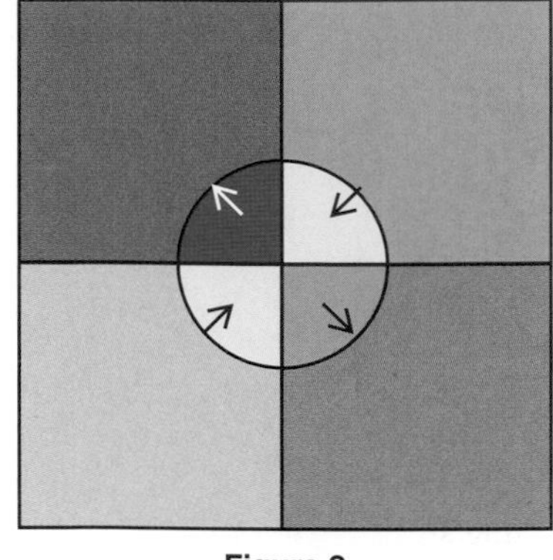

Figure 2
Sew blocks into 4-block units like this one.

5. Repeat steps 1–3 with (37) 6½-inch blocks and Template C and the 3¾-inch squares and Template D.

6. Refer to the Quilt Assembly Diagram (Figure 3). ***Note:*** *The quilt diagram is divided into large sections to piece together. Piece each section (A–P) first, and then join the pieces following the directions on the diagram.*

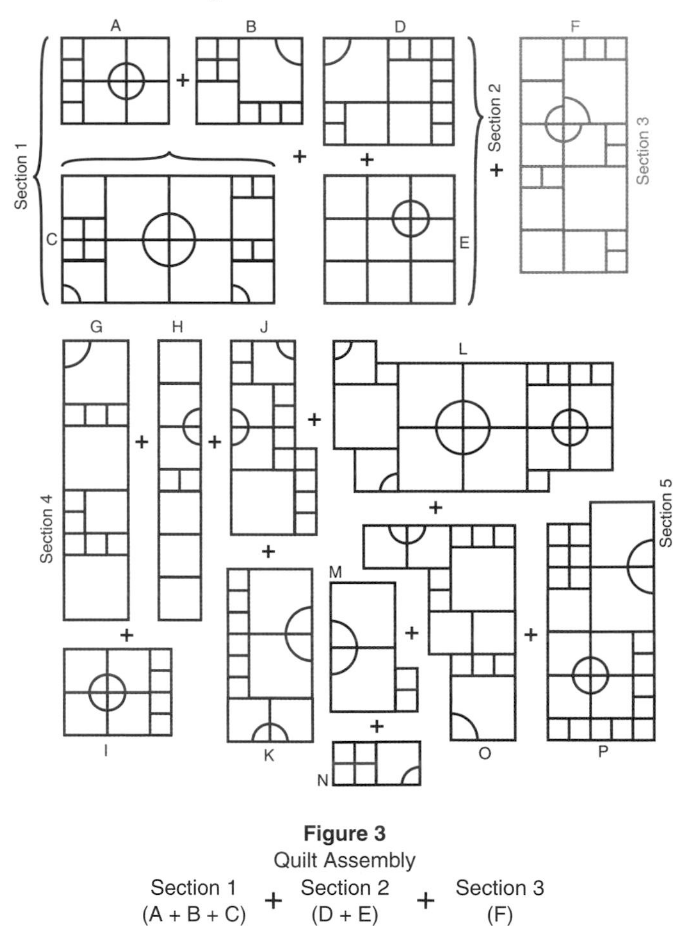

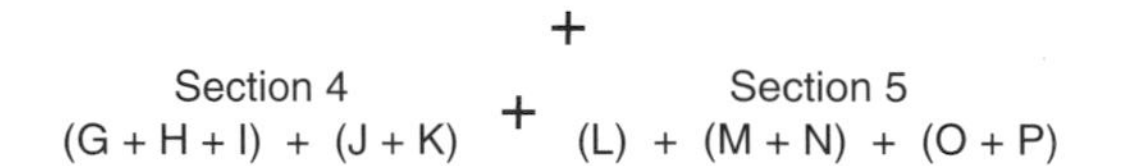

Figure 3
Quilt Assembly

Section 1 (A + B + C) + Section 2 (D + E) + Section 3 (F)
+
Section 4 (G + H + I) + (J + K) + Section 5 (L) + (M + N) + (O + P)

7. After piecing each section, sew the sections together in alphabetical order. Press the seams in one direction. In some areas you will need to sew inset seams.
8. To make the quilt backing, fold the backing yardage in half crosswise and cut into two equal lengths. Sew the pieces together, press the seam allowance to one side and trim to 72 x 90 inches.
9. Center the batting on the wrong side of the backing and add the quilt top, face up. Pin or hand-baste the layers together.
10. Quilt as desired. Trim the excess backing and batting even with the quilt-top edges.
11. Sew the binding strips together using bias seams; press the seams open. You should have one strip approximately 330 inches long. Fold the strip in half lengthwise with wrong sides together and press.
12. Bind the quilt edges using a ½-inch-wide seam allowance. Use a walking foot if available.
13. Wrap up this mocha treat and give to Dad on Father's Day. Add a label on the back with sweet sentiments, your name and the date.

CUTTING FOR PILLOW

Note: Preshrink and press all fabrics before cutting. Cut all strips across the fabric width.

- Cut four each of Template C and D (pages 30 and 31) from freezer paper.
- From the brown print, cut two strips 1¾ x 12½ inches, two strips 1¾ x 15 inches and two pieces 8¼ x 15 inches.

PILLOW ASSEMBLY

1. Use the freezer-paper templates for C and D as directed in step 1 for the quilt to cut the pieces for four 6½-inch-square blocks from the desired fabrics.
2. Assemble four blocks, as directed for the quilt.
3. Arrange the blocks in two rows with the quarter circles meeting in the center. Sew the blocks together in rows and press the seams in opposite directions in the two rows. Sew the rows together, taking care to match the center seams precisely.
4. Sew the 1¾ x 12½-inch brown border strips to opposite sides of the pieced pillow top. Press the seam allowances toward the borders. Sew the 1¾ x 15-inch brown strips to the top and bottom edges. Press the seam allowances toward the borders (Figure 4).

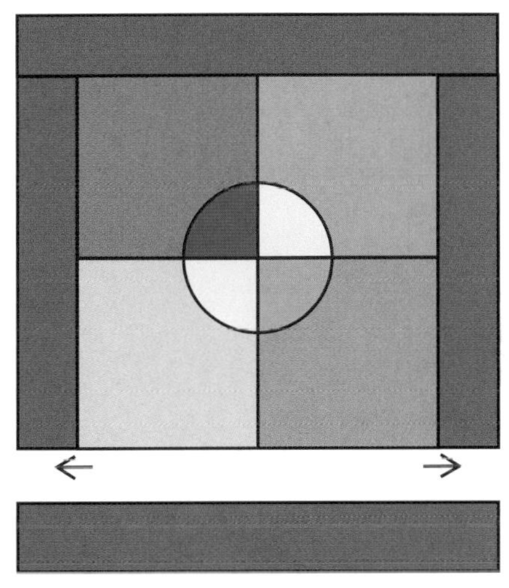

Figure 4
Pillow Top Assembly

5. Layer the batting between the completed pillow top and the 16-inch square of muslin and baste together. Quilt as desired.
6. Stitch ⅛ inch from the outer edge of the pillow top through all layers. Trim the excess batting and backing even with the pillow-top edges.
7. Using a ¾-inch-wide seam allowance, sew the two 8¼ x 15-inch pieces of brown fabric together along one edge. Stitch the first 1½ inches and backstitch. Change to a basting-length stitch and stitch for the next 12 inches. Backstitch. Return to the normal stitch length to complete the seam. Press the seam open.
8. Insert a 12-inch-long zipper in the basted section of the seam using a lapped application. Remove the basting and unzip the zipper.
9. With right sides together and raw edges even, position pillow back on the quilted pillow top. Stitch ½ inch from the raw edges. Clip the corners and turn the pillow cover right side out through the zipper.
10. Insert the pillow form and zip the zipper. ●

Make Mine Mocha

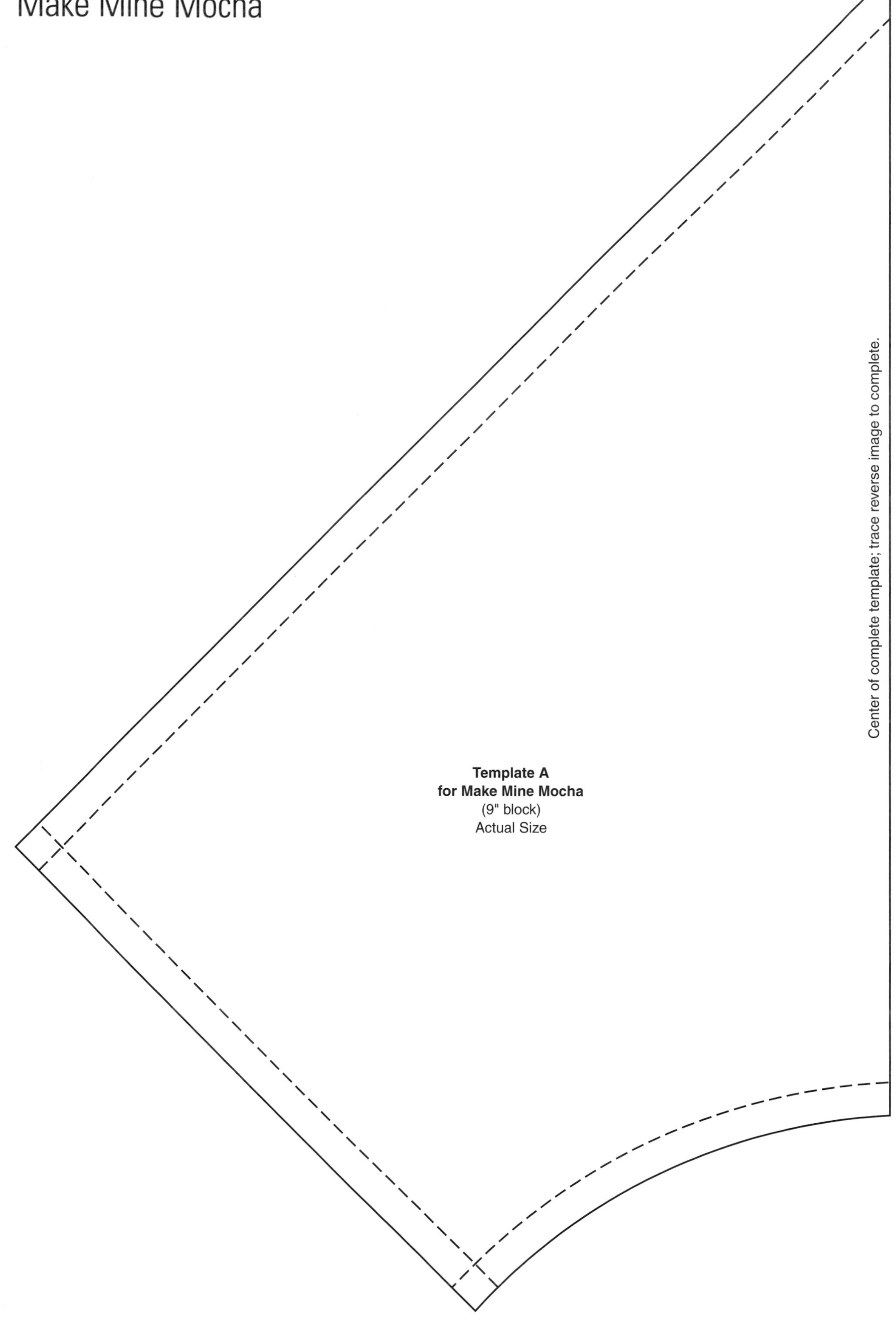

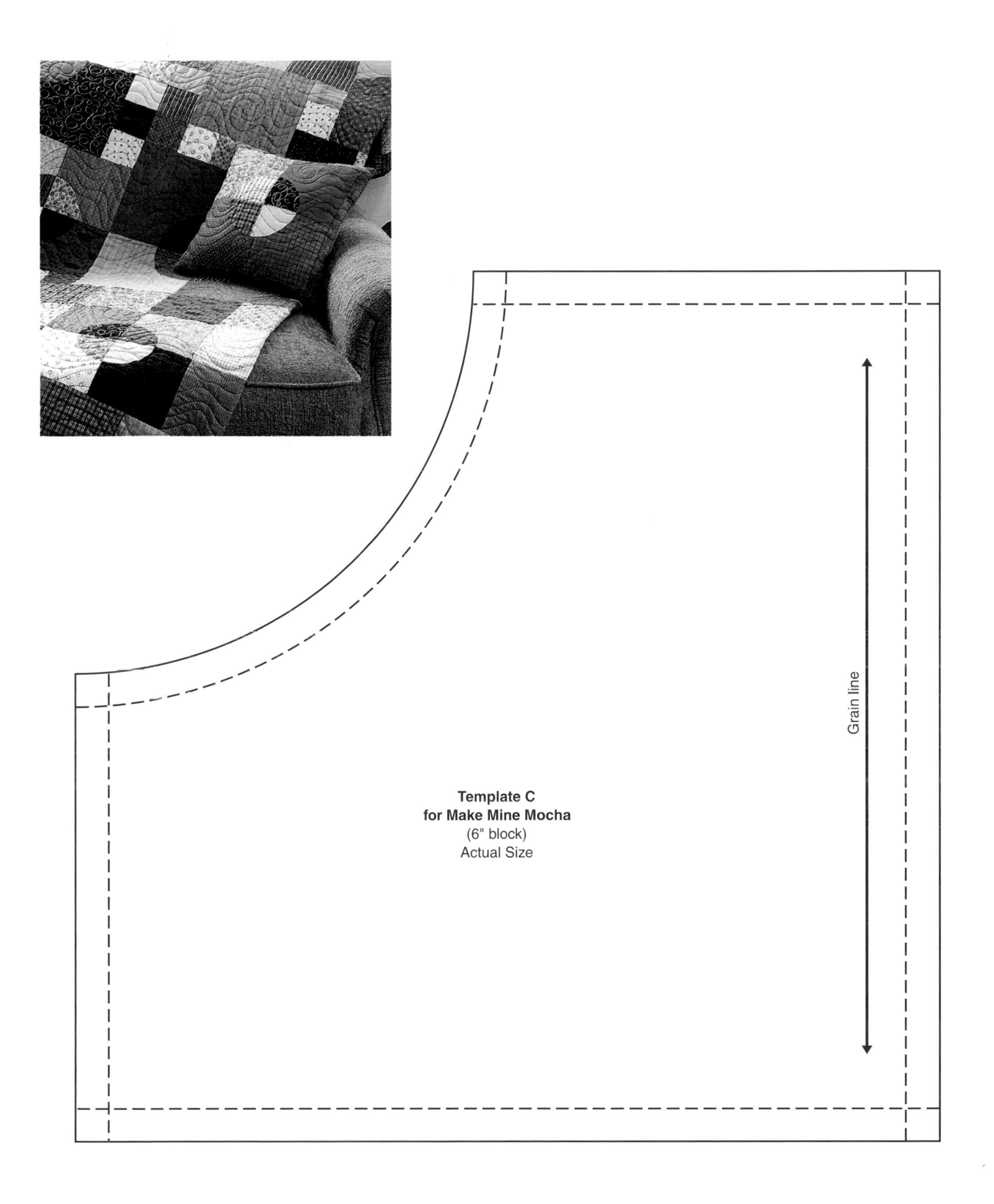
Grain line
Template C
for Make Mine Mocha
(6" block)
Actual Size

Make Mine Mocha

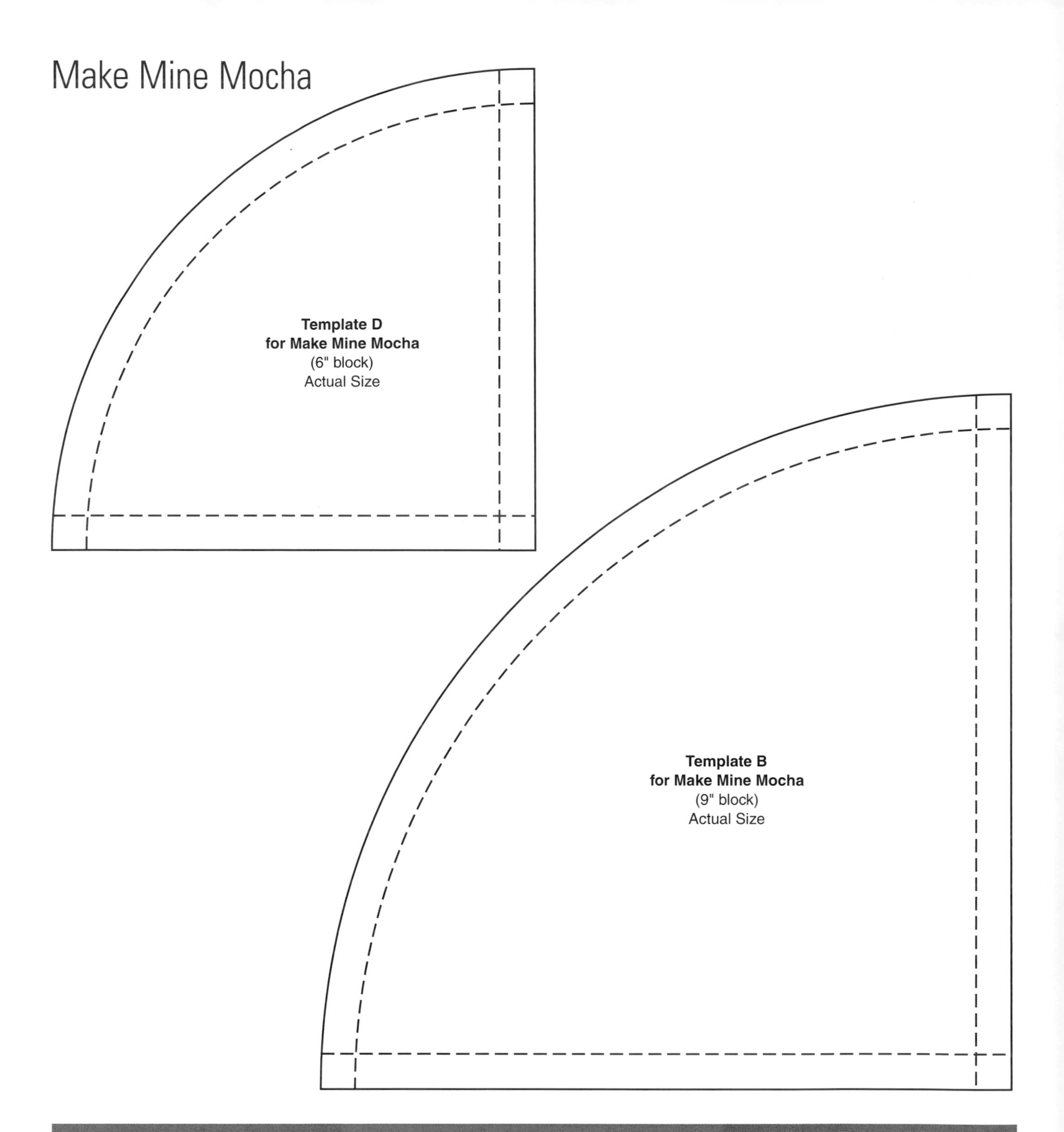

E-mail: Customer_Service@whitebirches.com

Fun & Easy Throws is published by House of White Birches, 306 East Parr Road, Berne, IN 46711, telephone (260) 589-4000. Printed in USA.

RETAIL STORES: If you would like to carry this pattern book or any other House of White Birches publications, call the Wholesale Department at Annie's Attic to set up a direct account: (903) 636-4303. Also, request a complete listing of publications available from House of White Birches.

ISBN-10: 1-59217-132-X
ISBN-13: 978-1-59217-132-3
1 2 3 4 5 6 7 8 9